Fountain of Life Publisher's House Catalogue

Scripture quotations, unless otherwise indicated, are taken from the *Holy Bible, King James Version*, Cambridge, 1769. Used by permission. All rights reserved.

Psalms 68:11 "The Lord gave the word; great was those of he company that published it."

The opinions expressed by the author are not necessarily those of Fountain of Life Publisher's House.

_____

Published by Fountain of Life Publisher's House

P. O. Box 922612, Norcross, GA 30010
Phone: 404-936-3989
Please Email Manuscripts to: publish@pariceparker.biz
For all book orders including wholesale email: sales@pariceparker.biz

Cover Design by Parice C. Parker

Interior Design by Parice C. Parker

Editing by F. O. L. P. H.

ISBN: 978-1542983181

Date: May 15, 2019

Welcome to
Fountain of Life Publisher's House

"Let Us Print Your Voice to Speak Nationwide"

Book Publisher's
Book Formatting
Website Designer's
Business Cards
Post Cards
Book Cover Designs
Editing Services
Letter Heads
Proof Reading
Book Reviews
Standup Banners
Magazine Advertisements
Catalogues / Brochures
& More

Visit Us Online
www.pariceparker.biz

Fountain Of Life Publisher's House

Welcome t0

Fountain of Life Publisher's House

Fountain of Life Publisher's House was inspired by Proverbs 14:27, A day that I poured my out heart to God. I asked him when I read this scripture I asked God, "can He to grant me a Fountain of Life?" Besides, through the gift of writing, I wonder if I would have denied that gift would I have a Fountain of Life? "No, I beginning writing music, and then years later I couldn't stop writing books. God multiplied my gifts of writing. Little did I know, it was in the bible Revaluations 1:11, "Whatever I show you write it in a book." I want other's to be encouraged to by the gift of writing. You will be empowered, inspired and entertained.

Proverbs 14:27 The fear of the Lord is a Fountain of Life to depart from the snares of death. We at Fountain of life Publisher's House has been doing just that, causing many to tap into their purpose, and live their dreams. Life is a joy and delight when you recognize who you are, what your goal is and fulfilling your missions. It is a powerful thing when one becomes an author. It grants them access while it multiples their opportunities, and blesses all around.

The power of perseverance brings forth evidence of faith. You would be surprised where your writing journey will take you and the doors that will be opened once you begin publishing. I thought I was going to write a book, and for years I worked on Aggravated Assault On Your Mind. It took me ten years because I kept stopping. However, one day an urgency took over me, and a flame ignited! I was sitting in church after this pastor had underhanded us out of our church, and was illegally evicted. So the following Sunday it was a beautiful sunshiny day. I was led to visit this church in Charlotte NC where I was currently living, and I sat in the back. I felt my life was all messed up. One minute I had a place to worship which was our church, then it seems in one week my life was turned upside down. I sat in the back of the church, and the Bishop came out in his black Bishops attire with his long cape, and he got on the pulpit and said, "God Don't Bless No Mess!" I was appalled because I was living in a messed up situation, and I specifically came to church for God to bless my life. I immediately heard the Holy Spirit say, "Go home and tell the world from Genius to Revelations that is My specialty. My purpose as God is to bless people Living Life In Messed Up Situations. My books were the seed of Fountain of Life Publishers House. See, where your gift will take you and how grateful you will be because of it. Let us help you become that author, and order some of our books, thanks for supporting our company.

CEO: Parice C. Parker

In the valley you will discover the potential in you, and a true warrior never get comfortable because they are always on the move to their arrival.

~ Parice C. Parker

2

Book: Mama I Heard Your Cry
ISBN-13 : 978-0991062737
Drama/ Woman Authors
Author: Chocolate Drop

Mama I Heard Your Cry Astonishing Award Winning True Story ... Day after day, struggle after struggle mama I Heard Your Cry. Mama tried through sickness, brokenness and heavy trials to keep our home as one. She never looked at life as what it really was. I often thought of Mama as a super Mom because she was so strong raising seven children, living a single life but married to a preacher that brought her more hell and strife. See, if they survived that disaster ...

$17.95

Book: Flawed
ISBN: 9781092521468
Non Fiction / General / Urban Drama / Adult
Author:

A down south Georgia girl that has been through it all - struggle, and pain. Rell left her to fend for her self-having to raise a child on her own. Dope Boy Eazy cheated on her with his so-called sister leaving, Peaches ready for revenge!

Betrayal in a way that will grip your mind and make you excited to turn the next page. Flawed is an urban drama and full of suspense, compelling you to complete this book in one day because Flawed will grip your mind while entertaining every second.

$16.95

Book : Anointing Powers of Your Hands
ISBN : 099044418X
Religion/ Inspirational
Author : Parice C. Parker

Often times you wonder why, why me? Your life may not look like much right now, but keep on putting your hands to the plow of your vision and do not stop, until you perfect & that thing! Working a work you have never worked can be extremely complicated and very difficult, but never quit doing the work. There is Anointing Powers in the working of your hands because He purposely created you. Faith without works are dead, so work on it!

$24.95

Book: Intentionally Single
ISBN: 9781093305203
Non Fiction / General / Drama / Woman's Author
Author: Laquanza M. Robinson

"Heartbreaks, sorrows, pains, triumphs, and a living sacrifice" were all made in the YES, Laquanza said unto the LORD. She has dedicated her life as indeed a living sacrifice for GOD to get all of the glory. Denying self of many pleasures to be molded, made and created by a higher power. A season of abstinence from sex and dating pulled her closer into the arms of a faithful GOD. Letting the strongholds be loosed by choice of living in the whole truth of her self-worth. Finding happiness within followed by, love, growth and her true purposed destiny. She tells the story of her tests, errors, and strengths to be a servant for Jesus no matter what she had to give up to be completely faithful. Loving herself into the will of GOD's willed plans for her changed everything that was believed to look like living life. Read her story of how she made an irrational decision to some that changed the course of her life forever.
$19.95

Book : Rise Above Now
ISBN: 0692723854
Fiction/ Contemporary Woman
Author: Shawn S. Martin

Have you ever questioned life and wonder why you? Can you hear yourself saying, Is there more to life than this? I can identify this with you. Did you know? Our brain process approximately 70,000 thoughts on an average day. Often any Wonder why so many give up and quit in life. In this book I will show you how to rise above mediocrity. No more settling for less than God's best and only fantasizing about your heart desires & It's time you Rise Above , Now.

$17.95

Book: My Purple MS Body
ISBN: 9781092586184
Poetry / Woman's Author
Author: Danielle Dixon

Bad things happen to good people. I know this to be true because I'm living proof! Living a golden diamond life is what all children seek as an adult life to come. As we grow older, the reality sets in there's more to life than what we see. As we age, the reality is that as a people, we are all different and must come together to reach, teach, and love one another for our differences. It's time to shake off the old. Intake the new of life is what God has for us, and make His reality our truth in the world of whom we as people are as God's children. Fight the powers of you because you only have one life, and make His dream come true.

$14.95

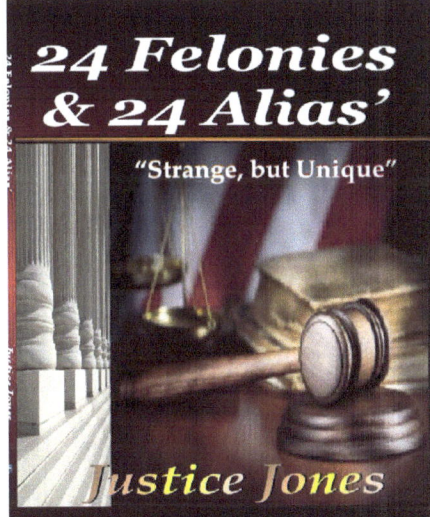

Books : 24 Felonies & 24 Alias
ISBN : 0692641823
Fiction / Crime / Drugs / Drama
Author: Justice Jones

A mother who looked for love in all the wrong places, combined with a father who loved crime and sex created an innocent daughter with both of those characteristics weighing heavily on her back. For we are people, created by two individuals whose DNA influenced greatly impact of my life we become. As I begin to put the story of my life out there, may God shine in the midst of a corrupt justice system.

$19.95

Book: Favor for My Labor
ISBN: 1537389793
Law/ Conflict of Laws
Author: Justice Jones

I was here during the era of The Missing & Murdered Children of Atlanta. There were no cell phones, and video cameras to record the evil activities, but I come to tell you anything you do in the dark will come to the light. Can't you see God is reveling it each, and every day? To do something about this, we must Get to the root of it, and the root must be uprooted. So therefore, I am going to do my part by unlocking the secrets that I have experience in the Blind Criminals Justice Systems because it was designed to make people look like career criminals.

$19.95

Book: Tragic
ISBN : 1546786538
Drama / Women
Author: Deidra Y. Del Angel

Ericka finds it hard to cope with the loss of her mom and baby sister. They were in a gruesome car accident that left her and two other siblings to disconnect over a period of time. Going from foster home to foster home, to living on the streets, Ericka was challenged every moment in her life thereafter. What is a teenager to do with so many bad choices in front of her?
$14.95

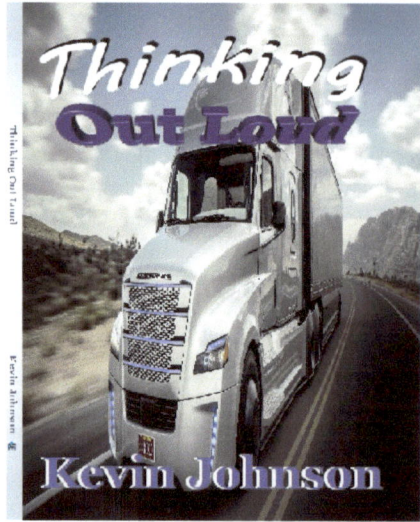

Thinking Out Loud
ISBN: 978-1546347781
Drama / General

Thinking Out Loud is about the people I met, the places I have visited and the eventful journeys that helped me to learn how to stop and smell the roses. Moving too fast is not always the best way to go. Some of the people that I had the pleasure of crossing paths with still hold dearness in my heart. Others, well some things are better unsaid. The places that I visited opened up my view of this great country of ours. Those episodes or should I say experiences again to lighten it up, helped me to get a better understanding of other people's perspective rather than assuming – I know what they are trying to say.

$25..95

"Understanding Grief"

Dr. Nichol Burris

Book: The Grieving Heart
ISBN: 1546478752
Self-Help / Death, Grief, Bereavement
Author: Dr. Nichol Burris

There is no right or wrong way to mourn or grieve the loss of a love one. You will never "get over" the loss, but you will learn how to move forward and build a new beginning. This is Your grief and "you're one step closer today than you were yesterday at becoming whole again."

$9.95 / B/W

Book: Revelations of the Heart
ISBN: 0991062701
Urban Poetry / Love Revelations of the Heart:
Author: Mirage

A fine collections of magnetic urban poetry … Words of lie spread as fast wildfire painted pictures of deception my heart is burning from hurt my tears falling forcefully trying to wash away the paint My breathe is fumed of smoke my soul is mixed up as the four season My voice cries out but the words are confused My hands are clinched in unity as my body is in the fetal position As I released the revelation of my heart from eyes of thorns to inspirations caused by pains and hurt.

$16.95

Non Fiction - Potent Books to Help Exhilarate You

Book: A Precious Gift from God
ISBN: 0978716256
Self-Help / Personal Growth / General
Author: Parice C Parker

Just when you think you have forgotten, and needing fulfillment, God will present you with a very special gift. A gift is typically given to you by surprise. An award is given to uplift, encourage, and packed with love. God worked miraculously, just to give you, and me the most precious divine gift of all. You will never know what all God has packed in this Gift. Unwrap it, and receive it with gladness in your heart. This gift is non-refundable and packed with shipping power from The Most High.

$18.95

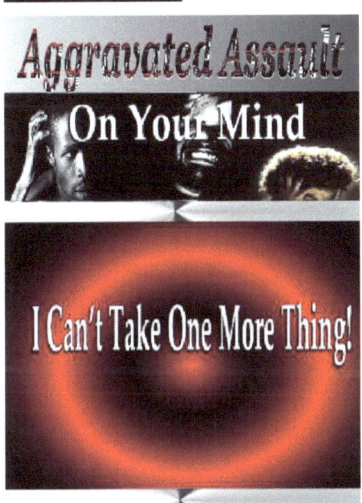

Book: Aggravated Assault On Your Mind
ISBN-13: 978-0978716233
Self-Help / Motivational & Inspirational
Author: Parice C Parker

When the very ones you have loved has MAXED out your kindness, taken advantage of your heart and turned their backs on you ... You are trying to do everything right, but nothing is WORKING OUT! Absolutely thinking, WHAT IS THE USE? Living life behind doors filled with chaotic issues, from the voice of a believer struggling to keep her sanity! I know you can relate. Is this what I have been praying for? When hell flood your LIFE & The STORMS continue to roar. This book concerns REAL LIFE issues! It is a MUST READ! Come explore how Aggravated Assault On Your Mind will chill your nerves.

$39.95

Book: From Eating Crumbs to Transforming Wealth
ISBN-13: 978-0990444169
Self-Help / Motivational & Inspirational
Author: Parice C Parker

From Eating Crumbs To Transforming Wealth: Anointing ... Finally, a book that keeps you in a thriving mental state that causes your HOPE to burst through! Now, it is time to identify the real you by introducing the TROPHY that is Hidden inside. It's your time to stop eating the crumbs of life and Indulge In Your WEALTHY Place!

$19.95

Book: Secrets
ISBN: 069273306X
Self-Help / Motivational & Inspirational
Author: Ernest West

It was the darkest place in my life where I contemplated suicide. I had lost my home, my family and I felt like a failure. I couldn't hold things together, and I let everyone down. I was living in a motel room.
It was dark and dreary, and I was all alone. I begin not to use my hands to right physically, but instead, I use my hands to write. My finger saved my life. I hushed and wrote. It was medicine, and in that place, my valley I begin to heal. Mysteries revealed.

$19.95

Book: Poems of Delight Ministering to Your Soul
ISBN: 0692745696
Poetry / Women Authors
Author: Sybil Young

What comes from the heart, reaches the heart& Poetry has always been a way to reach readers right where they need to be reached. The art of writing poems have caused many to fall in love with their purpose in life and thrive. Poems of Delight Ministering to Your Soul is a collection of poems that were truly written from the heart of author Sybil Young. Join her as she takes a journey through life, love and happiness and shares every moment with you through the beauty of poetry.

$14.95

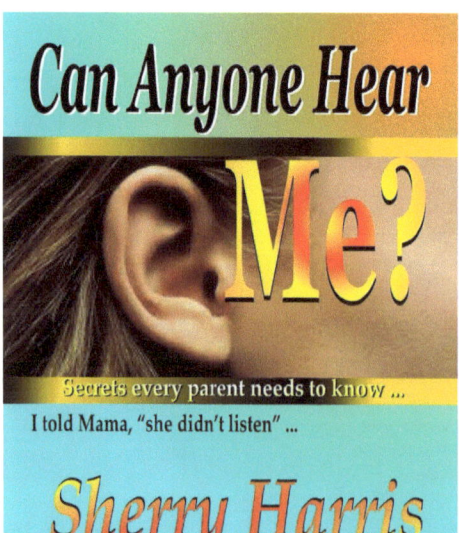

Book: Can Anyone Hear Me?
ISBN: 0990444104
Self-Help / Abuse / General

There are some things many will go through in their lives that may cause pain only to help others that shares t he same pain to be comfort in their time of trouble. For we have God that sets high and looks low. Yes, He does hear. Now, ask the question & Can Anyone Hear Me?

$12.95

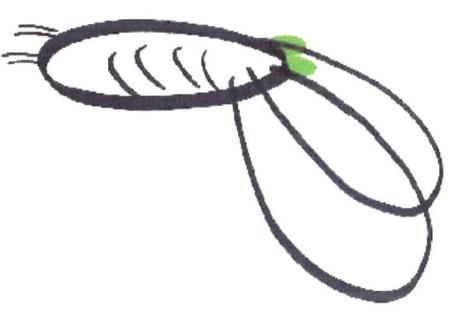

Book: Bria the Excellent Teacher
ISBN -1547147652
 Education / Teacher & Student Mentoring
Author : Marianna Culp

In our lifetimes, we'll run into a whole host of characters but none of them will make a more positive impression on our memories than Bria! She's on an ongoing quest to make members within the community polished by using fun and simple educational techniques. "Did you know that she assists all ages?" Yes, this is why Bria is so patient.

Her life is packed with action! Bria is always helping or leading in any way possible. While giving up, is not in her vocabulary, she certainly allows others to learn at their own pace.

Who knows where she'll be spotted at next but one thing is for sure, Bria is quite the professional!
$14.95

Illustrated by: Marianna Culp

Children's & Parenting Books

Illustrated by: Marianna R. Culp

Book: Ask an Elephant
ISBN - 9781724110602
 Education / Teacher & Student Mentoring
Author : Marianna Culp

What a busy week this elephant has! Dutch is known as an "Animal Idol" within his community! As a well-respected, hard-working and goal-oriented mammal, others are lead to communicate with Dutch. Everywhere he goes, someone is bound to run into him and ask a question. Well, Dutch is always prepared and polite to others. He gives educated answers and even interacts with a sing-along.

During his early childhood, his mother and father heavily encouraged writing, reading, listening and face-to-face interactions. This was the primary form of education in his small neighborhood called Chatters Estates. His family owned a business called A Hint of Communication. Because there were very little resources to get around to other parts of the larger communities, animals would come near and far to attend seminars to hear him speak as a young child. Dutch is a small town celebrity with great potential and humbleness. Dutch is a colorfully animated character who all can relate to.

Open the book and meet him!
$14.95

Book: HandiCAPABLE
ISBN: 0991062752
Comics & Graphics / Children
Author: Lisa Weldon

My name is Lisa Weldon. I am the author of HandiCAPABLE. I'd like to take a moment to introduce you to the main character of this book & named Lola. She is a five year old vibrant little girl who is wheelchair-bound. Lola considers herself to be a princess as opposed to being handicapped. Lola's wheelchair, better known as the & princess & mobile shows how much she loves anything to do with the princess theme. She possesses excellent qualities likes strength and compassion. Lola is wise beyond her years. In this book, we see how Lola's positive personality enables her to accept her circumstances, yet be hopeful about them changing.

$12.95

Special Needs Children's Books

Lola Goes to School
ISBN-978-1548987497
Author: Lisa Weldon

My name is Lisa Weldon and I am the author of the second book in the Handicapable book series, Lola Goes to School. As we saw in the first book, Lola is infatuated with anything to do with the princess theme. However, don't let that fool you. While sitting in her "princess mobile," she is sassy and spunky enough to stand up for herself and her friends. In this book, the main character Lola, along with three other children with special needs, courageously confront a group of bullies. The idea of this book is to show, that understanding and respecting each other's differences is possible and can have positive results.

$14.95

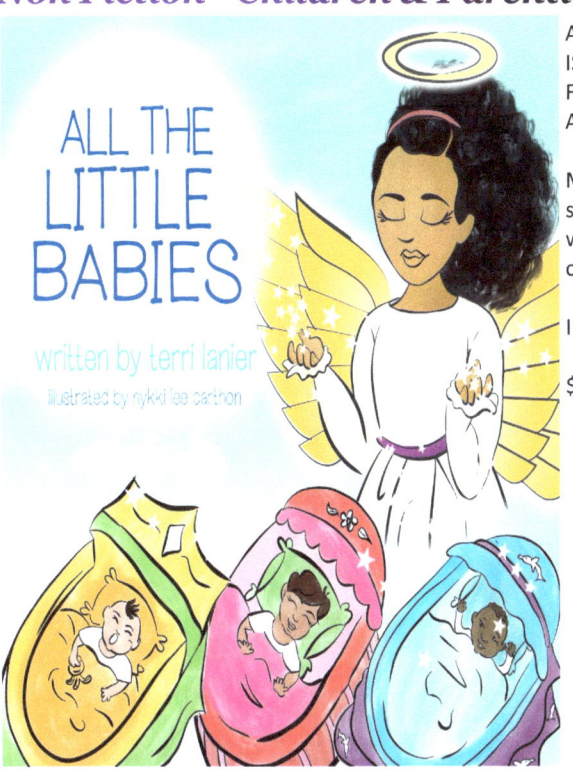

All the Little Babies
ISBN: 9781096587446
Family & Relationships / Parenting / Single Parent / Children
Author: Terri Lanier

My grandbaby inspired me, about seven years ago when I started babysitting and was given strict instructions on what I needed to do. I thought babysitting was a piece of cake. Oh, my, was I in for a treat?

I have the secret to help put your baby to sleep.

$12.95

Children's & Parenting Books

Book: Adventures with Chewie
ISBN: 9781097579129
Children's Book
Author: Wakiekie Reid

Adventures with "Chewie," will amaze every reader once they get to know Chewie because he captivates the eyes of the children; well as the heart of the reader. He is so smart and loves to help others learn what he knows. Let Adventures with "Chewie," inspire you and your youth; they will fall in love wanting you to read them more. Colors, shapes, and knowledge are what Adventures of Chewie readers will gain.

Where's Your Book?

Children's Books

Where's Your Book?

How to Write A Book Workshop

If you are tired of the old and ready for the new you? Register today for our next Writer's Workshop or our Book Writing Boot Camp. Becoming an author is exciting while it will introduce you to your purpose, define the real you and shape your destiny to perfection. There is an author inside every human being, but the choice is for you to produce what kind of author is in the inside of you, and write your voice to speak in print. Explore what's inside you by registering to become an author today.

www.pariceparker.biz

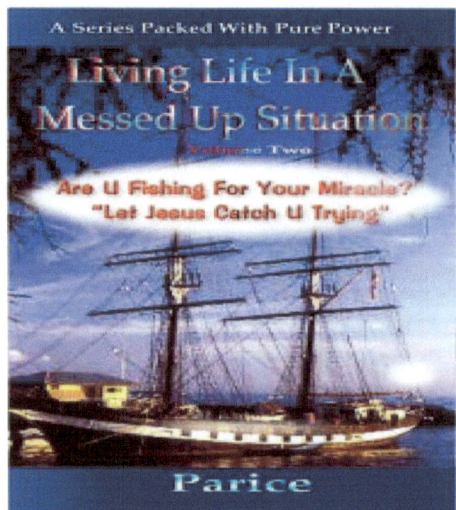

Book: Living Life In A Messed Up Situation Vol 2
ISBN: 9780978716226
Inspirational / Christian
Author: Parice C. Parker

Are you fishing for your miracle? Many are fishing and waiting on a miracle, ready but not prepared to handle it. If you want Divine Manifestation to appear in your life, this book is a must read!

$14.95

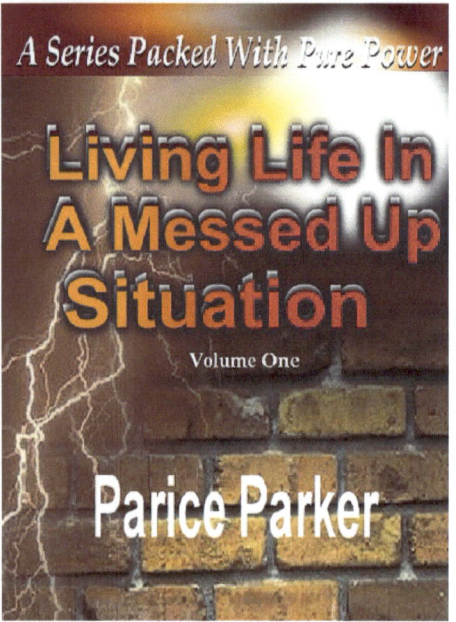

Living Life In A Messed Up Situation Vol: 1
ISBN: 0978716205
Religion / Inspirational / Christian Enthralling.
Author: Parice C Parker

One Sunday morning I realized my life was all messed up and I went to church sitting on the back pew because I did not want anyone to notice me. I needed a MIRACLE but the first thing the Bishop said, & God Don't Bless No Mess! It disturbed my spirit and Immediately I rose up and was inspired to write the book Living Life In A Messed Up Situations. God will assign the most in depth spiritual cleaning service through the Blood o Jesus the Christ to clean up your messed up life. Some things He dust off, others He wipes down and some needs to be POLISHED TO SHINE.

$13.95

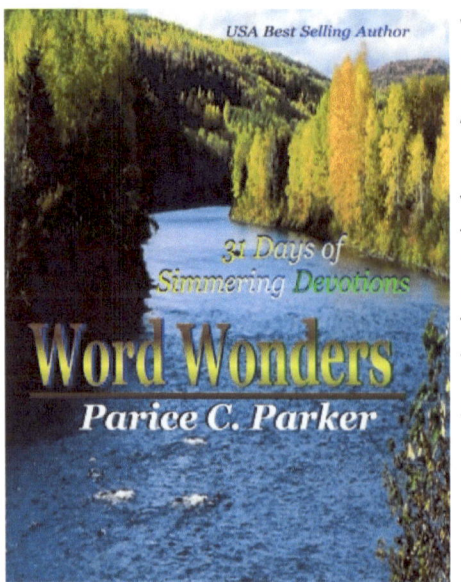

Word Wonders
ISBN: 0978716272
Religion / Inspirational / Christian
Author: Parice C Parker

Yes, life will throw many curve balls our way, and get us completely off track, and out of line with Gods will. You may not know when or how but He is going to answer you. Make your request known to your Way Maker, and be patient as you wait. When God's glory can be revealed to you, then you will be ready for all of your prayers to be answered, and not just a few. My question to you is, are you ready?

$17.95

Betrayal - Drama - Drugs - Suspense - Love - Hurt

Book: Born Into Brokenness
ISBN: 9781092738149
Non Fiction / General / Drama / Woman's Author
Author: Velicia L. Weldon

If you think you've gone too far, and you are too far gone that you feel like you're damaged goods. You may be the one that suffers from mommy or daddy issues? You have allowed your choices or bad decisions to govern your very existence. You're disappointed with life, and feeling you never have any wins. Life has dealt you a bad hand, but out of bad hands dealt you can still win. However, I stand before you calling you from the dead place! This season I challenge to you to level up! I call your unresponsive heart to beat again, and Born into Brokenness is a book you must read!

$19.95

Book: He's Incapable of Loving Me
ISBN: 9781798942741
Non Fiction / General / Drama / Woman's Author
Author: Katrina Renee

When you are tired of being single, you will make impulsive decisions. Loneliness can get you in trouble, and make you live dangerously! I thought I had to do something different. One day I decided to step out of the normal, and pursue a relationship on a dating website. Who would have thought that the relationship I thought was a blessing turned out to be a curse? The burdens that cost me emotional strain, self-worth and peace. If you have ever been in a relationship with someone that is toxic or have a narcissistic personality is a terrible danger to you. He's Incapable of loving me, is for you! This book will teach you how to push through traumatic experiences by examining, and taking accountability for your choices. He's Incapable of loving me!

$16.95

Book: I Surrender My Yes
ISBN:
Non Fiction / General / Drama / Woman's Author
Author: Tamika W. Edwards

Coming Soon!
$18.95

Grace Under Fire
ISBN : 0991062760
Drama / Woman Authors
Grace Under Fire is a Stunning Real Life Story
Author : Marilyn Leck

As a young girl, Marilyn had experienced more in her life than most children should at her age. In her distressing struggle through years filled with sexual, emotional, and physical abuse, she had to learn to overcome and cling fast to God in order to become free from the wickedness that had taken hold of her very existence. Grace Under Fire is a blazing story.

$15.95

The Woman In Me
ISBN : 0615848370
Fiction / Lesbian
Author : Miriam Passmore

What was I? I lived a lesbian lifestyle as a male impersonator for twenty years. I can remember as early as first grade, I had fantasies of being sexually involved with my school teacher. I was young and didn't Fully understand what sex was, but I knew I had a Problem. I became attracted to girls in my class but couldn't Tell my secret to anyone because I knew I should be attracted to boys. I was confused and afraid. I am human. I had an identity Crises and I escaped the gay lifestyle. A LETTER TO THE CHURCH/ A WITNESS FOR THE WORLD PEOPLE ARE SUFFERING IN SILENCE.

$15.95

The Assignment
ISBN : 0991062728
Religion / Christian Life / Inspirational
Author : Ace Ray

Are you tried of the devil messing with your mind and emotions? Your family is constantly faced with drama after drama and the enemy is attacking your body with your sickness and disease. It is high time to assassinate your enemy. When a predator like the Devil sees the light of the Father in you, he has to flee! It's hard for the devil to attack you effectively when you are busy doing the will of God

$9.95

Book: Get It Together
ISBN:
Non Fiction / General / Drama / Overcoming Depression
Author: Parice C. Parker

Life will trap you in a state of depression if you don't take control of it. People, things will easily persuade you to drift away from a good life and map out your life direction. Sooner or later you will be like a puppet with strings attached to your arms, and feet. Your situations, conditions, things, people; and sudden terrible life changes will begin orchestrating a new pattern for your life. Now, you are being led in another direction far away from the goals you planned, or decisions that would make your life worth living. It is time for not to allow anything or anyone else cause you to detour from your purpose.

$16.95
Coming Soon!!!!!!!!!!

Book: Breaking the Back of Poverty
ISBN:
Non Fiction / General / Financial/ Overcoming Poverty
Author: Parice C. Parker

Coming Soon!!!!!!!!!!

Keys to The Kingdom
ISBN: 0978716213
Self-Help / Motivational & Inspirational
Author: Keishan Scott

If God said it, then it is DONE! Going from the PIT To the PALACE is another way to receive Keys To The Kingdom. Once set in motion you have went down for the last time there is only one way to go and that is up! There are Key Points in Keys To The Kingdom you must know to obtain a profound relationship with The Holy Spirit. And, once obtained then you will gain Keys To The Kingdom. Once what was complicated is now easily accessed. A book inspired by God from the heart of a 11 year old Minister, and a child shall lead them!

$10.95

Way To Go
ISBN : 069274567X
Self-Help / Motivational & Inspirational
Author : Justina Nwukamma

I remember when I used to work as a charge nurse at a hospital. One of my assignments was assigning job duties to other nurses. If a nurse is disobedient, some consequences follow such as being written up and of course no one likes to be written up because it goes in the annual evaluation. Perhaps, it has been many known cases for faulty accidents that have caused wrongful deaths. Obedience is necessary, and it is practicing godliness in our everyday living just as cleanliness is next to Godliness. You will live a better life.

$13.95

The Superhighway
ISBN : 0991062760
Inspirational / Women Authors
Author : Phyllis R. Brown

Your angels are with you from birth they are there to protect and comfort you. Sometimes they come right out and talk to you. Other times it may be a small nudge or an intuitive thought that you wonder where that came from. Listen, your angels are trying to communicate with you. They bring you messages from God the Father and God the Son. He will also remind you of things that the Father wants you to know. God's messengers are our protectors and it's time you change your destiny.

$15.95

Book: Write-A-Holic -Dream Writer's
ISBN :
Self Help / Creativity
Author : Parice C. Parker

Write-A-Holic will contaminate you with an allergic reaction to being more successful, to end procrastination, and silence the drought along with getting rid of poverty from your life. If, you want to take better control of your life, and want to identify your purpose, then completely read this book Write-A-Holic. It will lead you on a more passionate journey into your destiny that will manifest your fate. Why live a life? And don't know who you are or find your passions in life? No more hiding, crossword puzzles with your life. Get to know what's in your heart, and follow it. Your heart will lead you to fortune.

$24.95
Coming Soon!!!!!

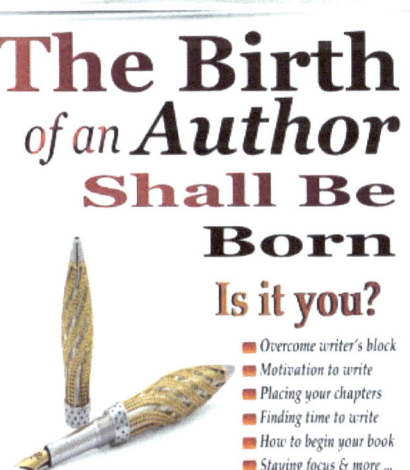

Book: The Birth of An Author Shall Be Born
ISBN - 13 : 978-0991062713
Self-Help / Creativity
Author : Parice C. Parker

There are great techniques for completing a book from the introduction to the end. An unfinished and unpublished book is dead. That book inside deserves to live. A lot of people wanted me to mentor them through their book writing journey because they witnessed how I have mastered book writing. The Birth of an Author Shall Be Born is purposed to get that book out of you . Push to give your new book an opportunity to live. Someone needs your book more than you need to write it. The Birth of an Author Shall Be Born, is it you? It's Time to discover the author in you and write your book.

$24.95

Book: The Birth of An Author Shall Be Born
ISBN:
How to Write A Book
Author: Parice C. Parker

 This Combo Package teaches one How to Write a Book, and together they will equip the writer to Master Book Writing Secret's to completing your book within less than 90 days.

$39.95

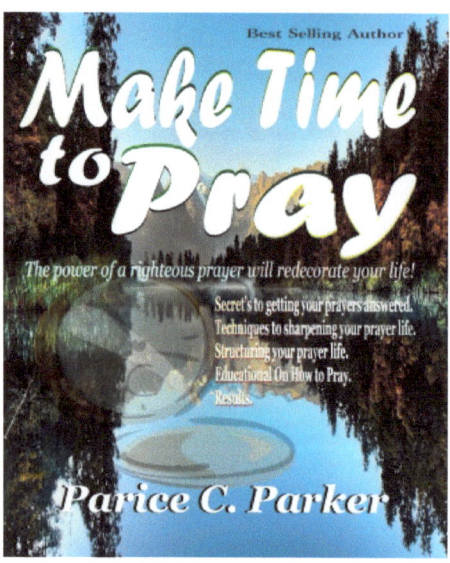

Book: Make Time to Pray
ISBN: 9781539382317
Christian Motivational / Contemporary
Author: Parice C. Parker

So many allow the struggles, discomforts, and evils of this life to redirect their lives from being viable because they don't know how to pray. Praying is the most valuable spiritual tool you will need, and it is a real weapon of defense when you learn how to use it. It will shift your entire situation from bad to good, redirect your life from misery to happiness and misfortune to being fortunate. Make time to Pray will teach you how to make your prayer more effective. Once an individual develops a more effective prayer life they become a hell destroyer, life changer, and a more productive warrior gaining favor from The Most High that they never had. It's time to Make Time to Pray.

$19.95

Book: Moving Forward
ISBN: 9781724071521
Self Help / Inspirational
Author: Juanita C. Jackson

Sometimes in life, when one door closes, another door opens. Yet, we spend so much time looking at the closed door, we ignore the open door of opportunity, love, and advancement. That's not the case for Juantia C. Jackson.

In Moving Forward Author, Juanita C. Jackson tells her courageous story of moving forward in challenging circumstances. While abandoned by her parents, she found the beauty in her warm and compassionate grandparent's who filled in the gap.

Her common-sense approach to moving forward is though provoking, refreshing, and invaluable to jump-starting your life. As I've said, "It's time to get Unstuck and follow, Move Forward and change your life."

~ Les Brown

$14.95

Book: Women It's Time for a Bubble Bath
ISBN: 978-0692708712
Self Help / Inspirational
Author: Delisa A. Johnson

Women, It's Time to Take A Bubble Bath will help people, reach their purpose, promise, and destiny. It is time to let go of past hurts, rejections, and drawbacks that have caused your self-esteem to be small. At the same time help you reach your full potential. You may cry, scream and shout, but you will never be the same because God planned greater for you before in your was in your mother's womb. This exercise will cause your healing to take place. And you will be able to help others. This book will change you and push you to your destination and promises. God had a plan that He wants you to fulfill, and you shall soar like the Eagles, roar like the lion, and the greatest part is that it will build your faith, trust, and confidence. Also, others will see the difference. Women, "It's Time Out To Take A Bubble Bath.

$18.95

CD Music: Somebody Say Jesus
Gospel Music
Author: Parice C. Parker

Anointing lyrics inspired by the Holy Spirit and relaxing to the soul as it sooths the roughness of life. Order your copy today

$13.95

CD: You Can't Overthrow This
Empowerment Messages
Author: Parice C. Parker

Powerful inserts to help boost your inner spirit to run, and not stop. It will cause you to shift gears and to press the pedal to the medal.

$14.95

CD: Thrust Me Into My Destiny
Empowerment Messages
Author: Parice C Parker

This CD encourages the heart not to give up and quit but it compels it to be thrust into it's destiny. You will never be the same after listening Make sure you order today.

$13.95

The Birth of an Author Shall Be Born - CD

1) Finding Time To Write
2) Overcoming Writers Block
3) Placing Your Chapters
4) Starting a Book
5) Stop Procrastinating
6) Knowing Your Readers
7) Tips Do Marketing Your
8) Book Scraps & No Much More ...

"Secret's to Mastering Vision Writing"
www.pariceparker.biz
Parice C. Parker

CD: The Birth of an Author Shall Be Born Workshop
Empowerment Messages
Author: Parice C Parker

The Birth of an author CD is a life recording of one of my How to Write A Book Seminar and you will learn techniques to crank birth the author in you.

$29.95

Book: Soaring Like An Eagle
ISBN: 978-1975680312
Christian / Poetry
Author: Laquanza M. Robinson

One woman's journey changed the moment she gave her feelings a voice, through poetry. Light after darkness, and freedom after pain. Eventually, all the hurt's produced beauty for ashes. Soaring above everything that was designed to stop her from knowing the truth. Every word of Soaring Like An Eagle came with a price, and it was tied to her future and the revelations of God's truth. It's time, you swap your sores, and begin Soaring Like An Eagle.

$15.95

Book: After You Say I Do Twice
ISBN: 978-1981650446
Non-Fiction / Drama
Author: Teresa Smith

Every girl dreams about her wedding day. We often are taught that getting married is one of the most important things in our lifetime. We are busy planning the wedding before we even meet our groom. We pick flowers, venues, the wedding cake, brides maids, best woman, food, music, colors, and hairstyles. We have big dreams for our marriages, say the traditional wedding vows, "until death do us part," and eventually the day comes … We have planned strategically for our wedding but not the marriage, but what happens AFTER I SAY I DO?

$19.95

Book: Look Again
ISBN: 978-0990444176
Christian / Poetry
Author: Sybil Young

Look Again is a book that will expose the secrets of moving forward in God. However, never make a hasty decision. By the time you finish reading this book of poetry you will have discovered the importance of looking again. Look Again will encourage your everyday walk of life. Once I saw what I thought was a picture of a vase, but as I took a second look from a different position., I saw two people facing each other. Wow, how I did I miss that? In this life there will always be a need to Look Again. Before you give up, Look Again. Look Again before you jump, do you know where you will land, then Look Again.

$17.95

Non Fiction - Books to Produce A Better You

Book: Intimacy with Abba Father
ISBN: 978-1978063228
Religion / Inspirational
Author: Tarah Manns

Out of darkness into the hands of God, was nothing. I had planned for or imagined it to happen, and when I was not looking for Him. A call to serve Him was vivid in my spirit. The beginning of a love affair that would change the course of my life and took me on a journey that is beyond the ordinary. If you're looking to go deeper in your relationship with the Lord or if you are a new Believer, and is unsure of how to grow your relationship? Intimacy with Abba Father is a perfect guide that will get you started on your new journey of a beautiful life.

$15.95

Book: Eye's to See Beyond the Valley
ISBN: 978-1981540556
Self-Help / General
Author: Andrella E. Williams

Eyes to See Beyond the Valley is produced to be a tool to facilitate a smooth, and swift transition from valley experiences by acquiring a deeper more meaningful relationship with the Almighty God and by being open, and willing to make necessary personal adjustments along the way. Finally, this book will offer techniques and principles that will compel the reader to look at valley experiences; the lows in life realizing that all things work together for their good. I realize that for the reader to see beyond their valley experiences or those hard places in life one must develop and nurture spiritual intimacy with God coupled with a sense of focus. One must be more than willing to adopt a change in perception. Every reader is exhorted to know that every power that existed to destroy us and rob us of what our God predestined for us has already been destroyed ...
$15.95

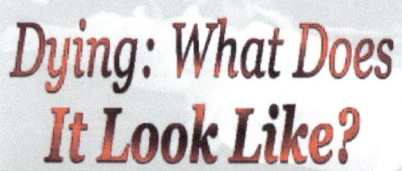

Book: Dying: What Does It Look Like?
ISBN: 978-1978127289
Self-Help / Death, Grief, Bereavement
Author: Dr. Nichol Burris

Dying has its challenges. The thought of dying poses many obstacles. Something that is so natural tends to stifle the very way we breath. We see it, yet we don't understand it! Death, like birth, is Universal. Death doesn't know age, gender, nationality, ethnicity, or religion. Sometimes we are able to plan for it, sometimes we ignore it, but either way we knowingly understand that it is inevitable.

$14.95

Book: The Grieving Heart
ISBN: 978-1546478751
Self-Help / Death, Grief, Bereavement
Author: Dr. Nichol Burris

There is no right or wrong way to mourn or grieve the loss of a love one. You will never "get over" the loss, but you will learn how to move forward and build a new beginning. This is Your grief and "you're one step closer today than you were yesterday at becoming whole again."

$12.95 / Color

Book: Celebrating the Colors
ISBN: 978-1978063334
Self-Help / Death, Grief, Bereavement
Author: Dr. Nichol Burris

Colors illuminate life and bring forth great energy. This book allows you to look at the beauty of the colors that make up our festive and joyous holidays. It also gives impacting and confirming scriptures from the New King James Bible to help affirm, and validate your faith during this most difficult time. Your faith has helped you during the course of life events and that same faith will help guide you through your hurt, and provide healing during the holidays.

$14.95 / Color

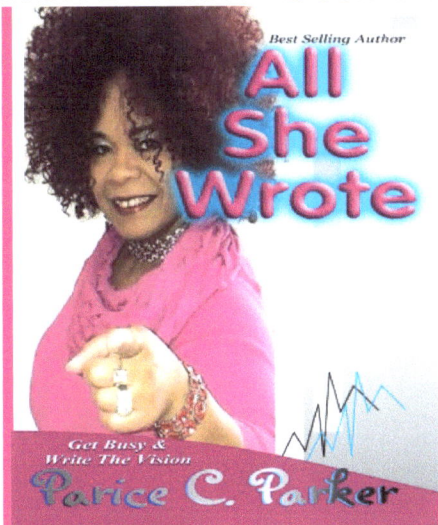

Book: All She Wrote
ISBN: 978-1981650170
Author: Parice C. Parker

All She Wrote is purposed to IGNITE a Flame inside you and destroy the spirit of procrastination once, and for all. Parice Parker is a POWER HOUSE author, and her books are very inspiring they have the power to cause the lame in spirit to run. All She Wrote is a collection sampler of Parice Parker's Anointed book collection that will help you with insecurities, push you to your purpose and possess your destiny. All She Wrote will cause you to move, live and exist. No more, lifeless life in All She Wrote. Order, your copy today!

$19.95

Book: The Sins of A Preacher
ISBN:
Non-Fiction / Drama
Author: Deidra Y. Del Angel

Daniel was next in line to fulfill the shoes of his grandfather walked in ministry, after his grandfather untimely passing. Nevertheless, young Daniel bit off more than he could chew. Daniel battled with all sorts of demons from his past; he still tried to push through despite all he was facing to keep his promise for pastoral duties. He soon learns that practicing what he was preaching was easier said than done. Young Daniel was a married man, with a beautiful family living the American dream until he laid eyes on the Jezebel that united a flame in his heart. Young Pastor Daniel realized that his grandfather footprints were no easy task when you had hell looking so enticing that it would make you dive in, quickly.

$19.95 Coming Soon!!!!!!!!!!!!!!!!!!!!!!

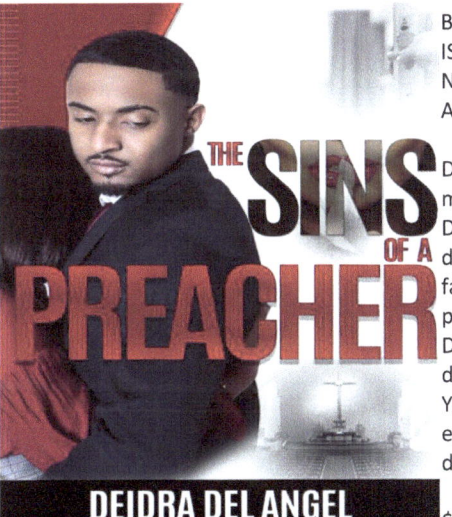

Book: Fountain of Life Publisher's House Catalog
ISBN: 978-1542983181
Author: Parice C. Parker

Your DREAM Matters and if you want to be a published author that's our mission. Though untimely things will occur and excuses will hinder your process but when you start with us then the spirit of procrastination dies. I Dream of becoming an author and for years I told everyone I was writing a book but one day I published and realized I made my DREAM come true. We want to help your dreams come true. The Birth of an Author Shall Be Born, is it you?

Our complete book catalogue with all out book titles, descriptions and services along with savings.

$9.95

Book : You are Unstoppable
ISBN : 0990444112
Self - Help / Motivation Inspirational
Author : Angela B. Walker

You are Unstoppable & is an inspiring book loaded with Revelation from God's word. Also, lessons from the experience of the authors journey in life, and ministry. Reading this book & You are Unstoppable is an opportunity to be illuminated , motivated, prepared, activated, challenged, and empowered. It is time to confront life with optimism, and a sense of mission in face of Adversity or insurmountable challenges! No matter what you go through in life you can overcome, and know that You Are Unstoppable!

$17.95

Book: Courageous Woman
ISBN: 978-1985806931
Body, Mind & Spirit / Inspiration & Personal Growth
Author: Antrionetter J. Meadows

Courageous Woman is a young lady going through treacherously, and she's having a difficult time trying to figure it out. Every day, she asks herself, "Why are things happening this way?" She was also trying to understand with all that she was facing that she needed a new strength to come out. She found a faith that was so courageous, and how she didn't let life or people stop her any longer. One day, she made a choice that forever changed her life, and her story is still being written ...

$19.95

Book: Cheryl
ISBN: 978-1978463646
Self-Help / Personal Growth / General

Author: Cheryl Buchanan
The darkness of hell, sex, death and witchcraft intended to destroy a life; becomes the music and light that thrives her. Love rescues her by this compelling story of overcoming will power that the dark forces was purposed to take her life out. See how Cheryl pushed against all odds, and who rescued her as she was drowning in the pressures life? Somehow, "Cheryl," knew it wasn't her end.

Hell is no match for life who believes in the love of Jesus because He has put His, "YES," into them, and from the beginning to the pseudo end, you will believe too.

$34.95

What Manner of Man Are Ye?
ISBN : 0991062779
Motivational / Contemporary Inspirational / Christian
Author: Catherine Rothwell

This book will help you discover places you have not even explored.
It's impressive in the manner it will direct you to umm ask yourself. It's time you be transparent with God, others and mostly yourself. Honestly is a rare commodity and What Manner of Man Are Ye will guide you to the truth. Jesus Said, &those that WORSHIP ME must worship Him in the spirit and in truth. Let & TRUTH rule your life by you beginning to um ask. One more question, how many things, opportunity or people you have to loose simply because you do not know who you was going be?

$15.95

Book: True Happiness, "the happiness that really got it going on."
ISBN-13: 978-0990444145
Self-Help / Motivational & Inspirational
Author: Rochelle Coleman

So many are searching in all the wrong places for happiness. Often people get excited as their emotions take ah old of the steering wheel of life, leading their lives into a wreck. Laughter in a moment of joy is not a true happiness but an outburst of good emotions. After awhile, your spirit begins to crash and joy comes tumbling down; putting your hopes in failing laughter and wondering why good things just don't last. Come and explore with me as I introduce you to real true happiness, something not made by man's hand.

$15.95

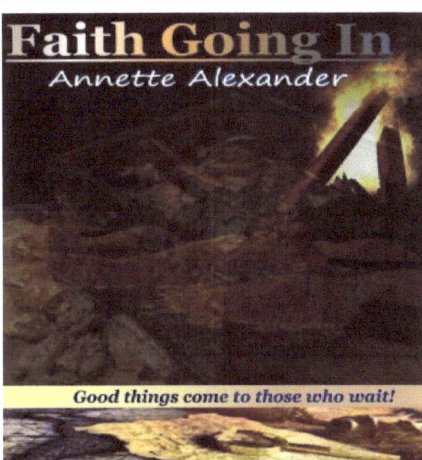

Faith Going In
ISBN: 0990444120
Religion / Christian Life / Inspirational
Author: Annette Alexander

Faith Going In: Terrific we dig such big holes and fall deep in them. Oh, how foolish? If you think for one second you can hide something think a little harder! What's done behind closed doors even the birds carry a voice which has wings and shall tell the matter.

$16.95

Non Fiction - Books to Produce A Better You

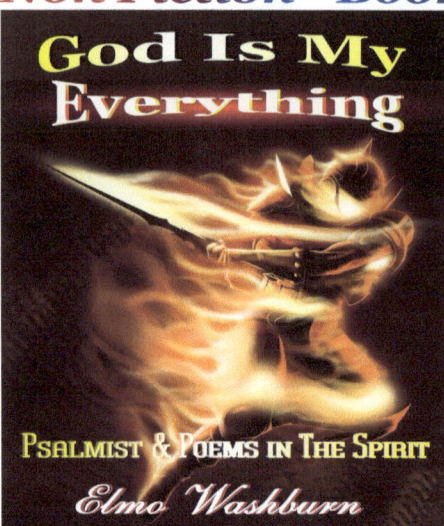

Book: God Is My Everything
ISBN: 9781719001984
Daily Devotional / Inspirational / Christian
Author: Elmo Washburn

I wrote this book because I love God, and He is my everything God has given me a beautiful gift to write so that others can be helped when they read it. There are so many who need help with songs, poems, and sermons. And, I love blessing people and helping others. My heart, soul, and mind are filled with the love of God to show, that God Is My Everything.

$14.95

Book: Power to Push You
ISBN: 0692667431
Body, Mind & Spirit / Inspiration & Personal Growth
Author : Parice C. Parker

Body, Mind , & Spirit/ Inspirational & personal Growth Militant Force ... When you fix your mind on the power to excel and purpose to hit the target, then it is a done deal. Your goal now is to achieve. No one, nothing or tiredness could stop you to be an eye specialist. Your eyes will begin to see the benefits of vision; the aspirations once accomplished, and you will have an IMPETUOUS ZEAL.

$24.95

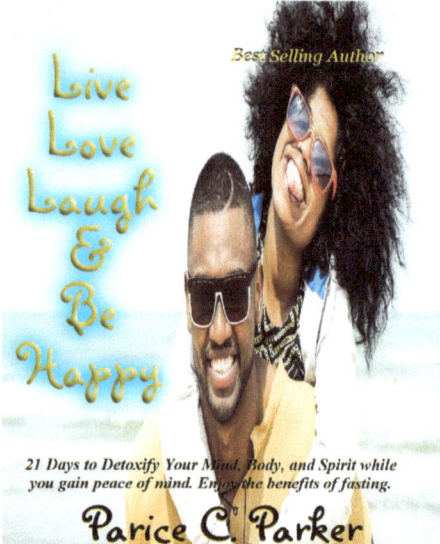

Book Live Love Laugh & Be Happy
ISBN: 9781726326384
Self-Help / Motivational & Inspirational
Author: Parice C Parker

To be happy you need peace of mind. Live Love Laugh & Be Happy will help redirect your thoughts, and help your mind to focus on the right direction. In life many chaotic things will happen, the issues of life will gets us off focus, and reposition our pathway of life; getting us off course. Live Love Laugh & Be Happy will realigns your life, and cause a fine adjustment to fix the things out of alignment, then you will gain a peace of mind, and get on the right track. Your life will attain happiness, real laughter, and peace. Get ready for the new you, as your read Live Love Laugh & Be Happy. It's time for you to enjoy every second of your life, and for you to be more productive.

$17.95

Book Magazine: Affluence Volume 1
ISBN: 978-1731019912
Self-Help / Motivational / Coupons / Health Articles ...
Author: Parice C Parker

Awe, a platform that's perfect to PRINT Your Voice & Vision in style. Affluence is more than a magazine, but a booklet in a series to push visions with a purpose, and increase the wealth of the visionary. You can share your business news, organization itinerary, share your products, music, testimonials, books, idea's, comedy, poetry, merchandise, place ads for coupons and more. Also, have your own column to build your voice to be heard. Affluence will help you introduce your vision to the nations; vending with high performance. Affluence is your money magnet. Advertise with us today, and gain more wealth tomorrow. It's time to go beyond the limits into an abundance of wealth, health and prosperity.
 $13.95

Book Magazine: Affluence Volume 2
ISBN: 978-1731450555
Self-Help / Motivational / Coupons / Health Articles ...
Author: Parice C Parker

Introduce your genre, life prospective's, idea's, creations and produce our cause with a voice in print. Affluence is the advertisement vehicle to generate you more money and to lead clients plus potential customer's your way. Marketing you in a business fashion making your vision more glamorous. Advertise your vision in style at an affordable rate. Affluence is ready to place your ad today log on www.affluence.biz

$13.95

Book Magazine: Affluence Volume 3
ISBN:
Self-Help / Motivational / Coupons / Health Articles ...
Author: Parice C Parker

$13.95

Place Your Ad Today

Book Magazine: Affluence Volume 1
ISBN: 978-1731019912
Self-Help / Motivational / Coupons / Health Articles / Fitness / Drama / Recipes? Beaty Secret's/ Hair / Crime / Love / News & More ...
Author: Parice C Parker

Awe, a platform that's perfect to PRINT Your Voice & Vision in style. Affluence is more than a magazine, but a booklet in a series to push visions with a purpose, and increase the wealth of the visionary. You can share your business news, organization itinerary, share your products, music, testimonials, books, idea's, comedy, poetry, merchandise, place ads for coupons and more. Also, have your own column to build your voice to be heard. Affluence will help you introduce your vision to the nations; vending with high performance. Affluence is your money magnet. Advertise with us today, and gain more wealth tomorrow. It's time to go beyond the limits into an abundance of wealth, health and prosperity.
$9.95

AMAZON & Where Books Are Being Sold

Place Your Advertisement Today or Subscribe Here

www.affluence.biz

404.936.3989

31

Fountain of Life Publisher's House

Inventory List Part B

Independent Sales Representative::

Representative Email:

Representative Phone Number

SHIP TO:

COMPANY NAME:

COMPANY ADDRESS:

Stock#	Author	ISBN	Book or CD Title	Price Per Unit	How Many	Total
BK -121	Parice C. Parker	0978716205	Living Life In A Messed Up Situation Vol 1	$13.95		
BK -122	Parice C. Parker	978-0978716226	Living Life In A Messed Up Situation Vol 2	$14.95		
BK - 123	Parice C. Parker	09787162272	Word Wonders	$17.95		
BK - 124	Catherine Rothwell	0991062779	What Manner of Men Are Ye?	$15.95		
BK - 125	Rochelle Coleman	978-0990444145	True Happiness, "the happiness that really got it going on."	$15.95		
BK - 126	ANNETTE Alexander	0990444120	Faith Going In	$16.95		
BK - 127	Marilyn Leck	0991062760	Grace Under Fire	$15.95		
BK - 128	Miriam Passmore	0615848370	The Woman In Me	$15.95		
BK - 129	Ace Ray	0991062728	The Assignment	$9.95		
BK - 130	Keishan Scott	0978716216	Keys to the Kingdom	$10.95		
BK - 131	Justina Nwakamma	069274567X	Way to Go	$13.95		
BK - 132	Phyllis R. Brown	0991062760	The Superhighway	$15.95		
BK - 133	Parice C Parker	Coming Soon	Write-A-Holic	$24.95		
BK - 134	Parice C. Parker	0991062713	The Birth of An Author Shall Be Born	$24.95		
BK - 135	Parice C. Parker	978-1539382311	Make Time to Pray	$19.95		
BK - 136	Parice C. Parker	Coming Soon	Live Love Laugh & Be Happy	$17.95		
BK - 137	Parice C. Parker	Bulk Book Collection	Power House Champion Book Collection	$310.00		
BK - 138	Dr. Nichol Burris	978-1973703433	The Grieving Heart Color	$9.95		
BK - 139	Dr. Nichol Burris	978-1546478751	The Grieving Heart B/W	$12.95		
BK - 140	Cheryl Buchanan	Coming Soon	Cheryl	$34.95		

Subtotal: _____
Shipping: _____
Tax: _____
Total: _____

Fountain of Life Publisher's House Phone: 404-936-3989
P. O. Box 922612 Norcross, Georgia, 30010
Email: info@pariceparker.biz Our Website: www.pariceparker.biz

32

Fountain of Life Publisher's House

Inventory List Part C

Independent Sales Representative::

Representative Email:

Representative Phone Number

SHIP TO:

COMPANY NAME:

COMPANY ADDRESS:

Stock#	Author	ISBN	Book or CD Title	Price Per Unit	How Many	Total
CD -1100	Parice C. Parker	Ready Now	Thrust Me Into My Destiny	$13.95		
CD -1102	Parice C. Parker	Ready Now	You Can't Overthrow This	$14.95		
CD - 1103	Parice C. Parker	Ready Now	It's Your Time	$9.95		
CD- 1104	Parice C. Parker	Ready Now	The Birth of An Author Shall Be Born	$29.95		
BK - 141	Parice C. Parker	Combo - Ready Now	The Birth of An Author CD & Book - Combo	$38.95		
BK - 142	Larry Simms	Coming Soon	Inspirational Thoughts	Coming Soon		
CD - 143	Parice C. Parker	Ready Now	Expressive Writing	$14.95		
BK - 144	Kareem Tomblin	Coming Soon	Your Daughter May Be A Thug	Coming Soon		
BK - 145	Michelle Fortes	Coming Soon	My Sister & Me	Coming Soon		
BK - 146	Parice C Parker & Grandma Rutha	Coming Soon	Black Man Stand	$19.95		
BK - 147	Kevin Johnson	978-1546347781	Thinking Out Loud	$18.95		
BK - 148	Tarah Manns	978-197863229	Intimacy with Abba Father	$14.95		
BK - 149	Parice C. Parker	Pre - Order	Breaking the Back of Poverty - Book	$27.95		
BK - 150	Parice C Parker	Pre - Order	Breaking the Back of Poverty - Journal	$12.95		
BK - 151	Parice C Parker	Coming Soon	The Pad Locked Church	Coming Soon		
BK - 152	Sybil Young	978-0990444176	Look Again	$15.95		
BK - 153	Laquanza Robinson	1975680316	Soaring Like An Eagle	$17.95		
BK - 154	Shior la queen	9781092521468	Flawed	$16.95		
BK - 155	Teresa Smith	978-198165044x	After You Say "I Do Twice"	$17.95		
BK - 156	Parice C Parker	CD	Make Time to Prayer More - CD	$12.95		

Subtotal: _____
Shipping: _____
Tax: _____
Total: _____

Fountain of Life Publisher's House Phone: 404-936-3989
P. O. Box 922612 Norcross, Georgia, 30010
Email: info@pariceparker.biz Our Website: www.pariceparker.biz

Fountain of Life Publisher's House

Inventory List Part D

Independent Sales Representative::	SHIP TO:
Representative Email:	COMPANY NAME:
Representative Phone Number	COMPANY ADDRESS:

Stock#	Author	ISBN	Book or CD Title	Price Per Unit	How Many	Total
BK-157						
BK-158	Dr Nichol Burris	978-1981650170	Celebrate the Colors	$14.95		
BK-159	Parice C. Parker	978-1981650170	All She Wrote	$19.95		
BK -160	Tarah Manns	978-1978063228	Intimacy with God	$14.95		
BK-161			I Surrender	$19.95		
BK-162	Dr Nichol Burris	978-1978127289	Dying: What Does It Look Like?	$12.95		
BK-163	Andrella E. Williams	978-1981540556	Eye's to See Beyond the Valley	$16.95		
BK-164	Parice C. Parker	978-1542983181	Fountain of Life Publisher's House CAT	$9.95		
BK-165	Elmo Washburn	978-1719001984	God Is My Everything	$14.95		
CD-200	Danielle Dixon	9781099262364	My Purple MS Body	$14.95		
BK-166	Juanita C. Jackson	9781724071521	Moving Forward	$14.95		
BK-167	Marianna R. Culp	9781724110602	Ask an Elephant	$14.95		
BK-168	Katrina Renee	9781798942741	He's Incapable of Loving Me	$17.95		
BK-168	Wakiekie Reid	9781097579129	Adventures with Chewie	$14.95		
BK-169	Terri Lanier	9781096587446	All the Little Babies	$14.95		
BK-170	Paice C. Parker	9781726730136	Affluence Magazine / Volume 1	$13.95		
BK-171	Paice C. Parker	978-1731450555	Affluence Magazine / Volume 2	$13.95		
BK-172	Paice C. Parker	9781099459290	Affluence Magazine / Volume 3	$13.95		
BK-173	Velencia Weldon	9781092738149	Born Into Brokenness	$17.95		
BK-174	Laquanza Robinson	9781093305203	Intentionally Single	$17.95		

Subtotal: _____
Shipping: _____
Tax: _____
Total: _____

Fountain of Life Publisher's House Phone: 404-936-3989
P. O. Box 922612 Norcross, Georgia, 30010
Email: info@pariceparker.biz Our Website: www.pariceparker.biz

Fountain of Life Publisher's House

Inventory List Part D

Independent Sales Representative::

Representative Email:

Representative Phone Number

SHIP TO:

COMPANY NAME:

COMPANY ADDRESS:

Stock#	Author	ISBN	Book or CD Title	Price Per Unit	How Many	Total
BK-157						
BK-158	Dr Nichol Burris	978-1981650170	Celebrate the Colors	$14.95		
BK-159	Parice C. Parker	978-1981650170	All She Wrote	$19.95		
BK -160	Tarah Manns	978-1978063228	Intimacy with God	$14.95		
BK-161			I Surrender	$19.95		
BK-162	Dr Nichol Burris	978-1978127289	Dying: What Does It Look Like?	$12.95		
BK-163	Andrella E. Williams	978-1981540556	Eye's to See Beyond the Valley	$16.95		
BK-164	Parice C. Parker	978-1542983181	Fountain of Life Publisher's House CAT	$9.95		
BK-165	Elmo Washburn	978-1719001984	God Is My Everything	$14.95		
CD-200	Danielle Dixon	9781099262364	My Purple MS Body	$14.95		
BK-166	Juanita C. Jackson	9781724071521	Moving Forward	$14.95		
BK-167	Marianna R. Culp	9781724110602	Ask an Elephant	$14.95		
BK-168	Katrina Renee	9781798942741	He's Incapable of Loving Me	$17.95		
BK-168	Wakiekie Reid	9781097579129	Adventures with Chewie	$14.95		
BK-169	Terri Lanier	9781096587446	All the Little Babies	$14.95		
BK-170	Paice C. Parker	9781726730136	Affluence Magazine / Volume 1	$13.95		
BK-171	Paice C. Parker	978-1731450555	Affluence Magazine / Volume 2	$13.95		
BK-172	Paice C. Parker	9781099459290	Affluence Magazine / Volume 3	$13.95		
BK-173	Velencia Weldon	9781092738149	Born Into Brokenness	$17.95		
BK-174	Laquanza Robinson	9781093305203	Intentionally Single	$17.95		

Subtotal: _____
Shipping: _____
Tax: _____
Total: _____

Fountain of Life Publisher's House Phone: 404-936-3989
P. O. Box 922612 Norcross, Georgia, 30010
Email: info@pariceparker.biz Our Website: www.pariceparker.biz

The Benefits of Prayer

To all that need more prayer, and understand the purpose of prayer or need to know how to pray. *Make Time to Pray* will inspire one to desire to pray, and look forward to building a genuine prayer life with the Holy Spirit.

You cannot allow ANY SPIRIT SPEAK OVER YOUR LIFE and PREACH into your hearing! It could be DEADLY and TOXIC to your spirituality that is why it is so many walking dead today because they hooked up with the wrong people. Everyone that carries the cross is moving for a different purpose, and he or she is not of Jesus the Christ. Whatever ANOINTING & Spirituality that is inside of them shall soon POSSESS you, and DRESS YOUR ATMOSPHERE as it prepares your destiny. Inquire of the LORD before you connect with people. I know this exact phrase is not in the bible, but it means the same thing, "Try the Spirit By the Spirit." If you DON'T Agree then why are you fellowshipping with Spirits that are not RIGHTEOUS?

So many don't realize the value of your connections because it will feed your life or suck it right out of you. Many people are walking spiritual dead appearing as zombies with their faith just because of the wrong people with the wrong motives in their life. Everyone has an incentive to connect with you make sure you know their reasons. I use to allow anyone in my life because of ministry trying to be useful to all and one day I woke up living in hell doing good. Yes, even in doing good things life can turn upside down and inside out. So, therefore, I had to recheck everyone's motive in my life. One by one I begin to access their purpose. A few valuable questions you must ask and answered yourself:

There are powerful benefits you will inherit once you are made more aware of the effectual powers of a powerhouse prayer warrior. You simply need answers and how to gain more spiritual knowledge in life. So that your life will be better productive, and you will become more at peace with your life. *Make Time to Pray* is an essential, and very resourceful book that needs to be added to your daily library to enhance your communication skills with our Heavenly Father for you to inherit all you are destined to.

DEFINITION OF *PRAYER*

1. A devout petition to god or an object of worship.
2. A spiritual communion with god or an object of worship, as in supplication, thanksgiving, adoration, or confession.
3. The act or practice of praying to god or an object of worship.
4. A formula or sequence of words used in or appointed for praying:
The Lord's prayer.
5. Prayers, a religious observance, either public or private, consisting wholly or mainly of prayer.
6. That which is prayed for.
7. A petition; entreaty.

So many people don't understand the purpose of prayer, and many think it's just a ritual or a tradition. There is so much power in prayer when it's effective. It is a way of communication to our Heavenly Father connecting to Him spiritually, and through our open discussion of exercising prayer. We can download anointing power that will add light to a dark place, give knowledge that will instruct wisdom to be evident in our lives, and replace curses for a blessing. Don't you want to live a more effective and productive life? Prayer literally will transform your life in a blink of an eye. It is definite to be a life changer. We all need prayer, and with the power of prayer, your life will be transformed, but you must begin by *Make Time to Pray*.

Praying is a necessity to any conquers and the greatest failures. I realized that through prayer has empowered me to get back up, and run to see what my end, shall be. Life is not easy but it can be dazzling with goodness if you learn the power of prayer. If you need power in a hopeless situation just make time to pray. If you ever get in over your head just make time to pray and when you are really tired of losing out on life opportunities just make time to pray. In this book *Make Time to Pray* you will be enthused with generous power so that your life conditions will be more peaceful, happy, flowing with goodness and impacting lives to be inspired with a fresh ray of hope.

Only $299.00 Get You Started!

Book Publishing

__Psalms 68:11 God gave the word but Great was those of the company that published it.__

Book publishing is a serious journey but PLEASURABLE on too. We CONGRATULATE YOU for your determination, dedication, perseverance, and accomplishing this challenging endeavor. We Want To *HELP YOU* Become A **SUCCESSFUL AUTHOR!** Now, it's time You Proceed in getting Your New Book Published and WE ARE THE BEST! We offer Book Publishing Packages that will best benefit our authors where they will be READY TO GO with all their marketing and vending supplies. We are currently offering GREAT SPECIALS just **LOCK IN TODAY**, pick and choose the package that best fit your needs. **Are You Ready?**

"Discover the Author In You Book Writing Camp"

Our writer's Discover the Author In You Book Camp will help you produce your NEW BOOK. It will teach you writing techniques to master book writing, keep you focused, and fueled with intense motivation. You will learn strategies for book writing, gain creative impartation and develop secrets to developing the best writer to birth out of you. It is a four-day empowerment hands on training class. You will be motivated to finished. Are you ready to become the next NEW YORK TIMES BEST SELLING AUTHOR or your book be the next BOX OFFICE HIT MOVIE? Please ask your sales representative how to register for our next class or just visit our website at www.pariceparker.biz. The Birth of an Author Shall Be BORN, IS IT YOU?

BOOK news

Issue 2, August 2019

Fountain of Life Publisher's House & Affluence Magazine, INC.

ALL THE LITTLE BABIES

written by
terri lanier

illustrated by
nykki lee carthon

monthly newsletter

Affluence Magazine

What's New

My grand baby inspired me, about seven years ago when I started babysitting and was given strict instructions on what I needed to do. I thought babysitting was a piece of cake. Oh, my, was I in for a treat?

Amazon & Where Books Are Being Sold

To place your ad with Affluence Magazine

1) Email your advertisement to affluenceadvertiseme@gmail.com

2) $AffluenceMagazine (Please Cash App your donation here)

3) Any question call 404.936.3989 www.affluence.biz

Content

Author Be INSPIRED to Write More ...

Book Writing is more than storytelling; it also enhances lives through reading the climaxes, inspiration, and even demonstrating the negatives which inmost case's some can relate. So many well-known authors begin writing due to various reasons, never expecting their books to take off as they did. Nevertheless, as they wrote their lives eventually was upgraded during their perseverance and, the working of their hands. Author, C. J. Lions was one of the authors that weren't expecting to sell a million copies, but she wanted to write, which was her dream. Learn to believe in yourself and write it out. You would be amazed at your results. In book writing, you must find your writing style and begin to write more. Writing is something you must perfect through practice, and the more you write, the better you will become. You want more than write more. Why quit at just one or two books. It took Author, C. J. Lions about four books before she made it. Get back on your writing journey and produce your New York Times Best Seller.

FOUNTAIN OF LIFE PUBLISHER'S HOUSE & AFFLUENCE MAGAZINE 404.936.3989 WWW.PARICEPARKER.BIZ

Now Hiring Independent Sales Consultants

Fountain of Life Publisher's House has opportunities waiting for you to increase your wealth, upgrade your life securities and transform your financial status. We are now hiring Independent Sales Contractors for our Book Catalog which is our newest edition, **Affluence** or booklet magazine. Affluence will be an excellent source for business owners to transform their business ideas, news, promotions, and visions. **Affluence** is the purpose of promoting business owners visions in style! You can make at least $25.00 per hour with just one sale per hour. Now, think about $25.00 times 4= $100.00 times five days a week working part-time. You can make $500.00 per week or more. What could you do with $500.00 per week? Apply Today online.

Requirements:
Must Be Neat & Clean
Have a Friendly Personality
Good Customer Service Skills
Submit Your Online Application
A Working Cell Phone or Contact Number
Desiring to Make at Least $25.00 Per Hour

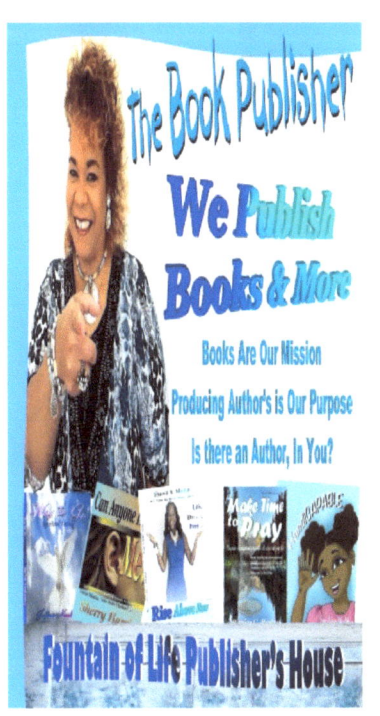

Advantages:
You Can Earn $250.00 - $3600.00 + Monthly or more
Flexible Hours - You Choose Your Own Hours
Take The Limits Off Your Money $$$$$$
Work From Your Phone orb Home
Earn Awards
Win Prizes

Please apply online
www.pariceparker.biz then click Job /Career

We Build Web Sites Too

Business On The Go Package

Start Your Business Today - Text I'm Ready to Start My Business 404.936.3989

1) Standup Banner w/ Carrying Case
2) 1000 Business Cards
3) 500 Postcards
4) A Professional Website Design
5) EIN & More

Open Your Account Today!

No Credit Check

Guaranteed Approval w/ $250.00 Deposit

www.pariceparker.biz

Call Today Phone: 404-936-3989

Fountain of Life Publisher's House P. O. Box 922612 Norcross, Georgia, 30010

Fountain of Life Publisher's House

P. O. Box 922612 Norcross, Georgia, 30010

Email Your Manuscript to info@pariceparker.biz

Phone: 404-936-3989

www.pariceparker.biz